Soldier, Sailor, Skipper

David Collinson

Shield Crest

ISBN 978-1-913839-22-2

MMXXI

A CIP catalogue record for this book
is available from the British Library

Published by
ShieldCrest
Aylesbury, Buckinghamshire, HP18 0TF
England
www.shieldcrest.co.uk
+44 (0) 333 8000 890

To Michael,

Our beloved son

THE AUTHOR

David Collinson comes from a shoe making and retailing background. His family shoemaking business began in 1811. He is married to Alison and they have two children. Tragically, their first child, Michael, to whom this book is dedicated, never recovered from a heart operation at the age of 14. Their second son now works for the London Fire Service and their daughter is a heart nurse. They feel lucky to also have two great grandchildren, a girl and a boy.

The book deals with most of his sailing experience but mingled with his sailing was a career in the army. He was assigned to the Kings Liverpool Regiment but later posted to the 1st Battalion of the South Lancashire Regiment, which at that time was serving in the Free State of Trieste. From Trieste posted to the Sudan and Khartoum he enjoyed sailing and was in charge of the Signals Platoon, responsible for all the communications for the Battalion.

He has never regretted his Army Service as it was a wonderful opportunity to visit many places which he otherwise would never have seen.

EARLY DAYS

I suppose everything starts in a small way. When in WW2, I was evacuated to the beautiful seaside town of Criccieth in North Wales, playing about in the sea was a daily pastime. It did not take long before my friend Errol Williams and I – both aged about eight – wanted to start sailing. We managed to find a small flat-bottomed dinghy; one of the problems we experienced was that it was just blown sideways, so the answer must be some sort of keel. We attached a small piece of wood to the bottom of the dinghy, but since we were launching from the beach, it had to fold flat on hinges and then be pulled down by ropes when floating in enough water. This caused us endless fun but was not at all effective. So was born *HMS Patchwork*. Our sailing adventures were greatly spurred on by the most enjoyable books written by Arthur Ransome—we read them all.

Dinghy Sailing

Sailing is an odd hobby, not as you think it might be, sitting in the sun enjoying a gentle breeze, oh no, that's just a dream. You have to be able to scrub, clean, and sand the bottom of a yacht, then antifoul the bottom, so it helps to be handy with a paintbrush before you start polishing the topsides, and that's just for starters. You need to be a bit of a mathematician if you are to navigate properly using a sextant, without a GPS. If you are on the way to the Mediterranean, it does help to speak a little French, Spanish, Portuguese, and Italian. There is the engineering too, so you can maintain the engine working in very small and tight spaces, attend to the electrics, fix the loo, understand meteorology, be a carpenter, negotiate with customs and marina officials, pass your Yachtmasters and radio exams, and I nearly forgot the most important skill of all, do the cooking. That is, of course, even before you start to sail!

ARMY DAYS

My sailing carried on during holidays on the Norfolk Broads until I joined the army, and somehow the officer in charge of a party detailed to clean a collection of dirty boats spotted me and said, "You are interested in sailing; you can clean the bottom of this boat." I had not volunteered, you never do in the army, but he must have done his homework and knew. How wonderful it all turned out, for when the yacht was cleaned and made good, he said, "That yacht is yours for as long as you are posted here."

Bottom Cleaning on the Nile

It turned out that there was a British Services Sailing Club on the Blue Nile in Khartoum, and the yachts were moored there. The yacht granted to me was a 14-foot metal dinghy named *Andromeda*, Bermudan rigged and made of metal because of all the wood-boring insects. There was another class of 18 footers; both were heavy by modern standards, but since you are all racing on level terms, it made little difference. The sailing club was housed in an old river ferry and was quite big. It had been filled with concrete to make it waterproof. We had a devoted Sudanese steward,

Racing 14 foot metal yachts

who looked after us and rowed us out to the dinghies moored in the river.

Our days started very early in the morning to avoid the midday and afternoon heat, so our duties were finished by lunchtime. This schedule allowed us to walk down to the river and go sailing most afternoons. Often, we would sail up under the Blue Nile Bridge to Crocodile Island and watch the beasts slip into the water in the hope of a meal, then at weekends, there would be racing. Rank played little part in the proceedings. Even the Regimental Sergeant Major had to give 'water at the mark' when asked! Occasionally, we would sail down the Blue Nile to its confluence with the White Nile, turn left and sail up the White Nile to an old flying boat base, and there we would have a series of races.

I never understood why we sailed there, but it was fun and maybe more convenient to the RAF base near there. The boys in blue were very good sailors and were often winners, but I must have done something right, for here is a picture of a medal that was awarded to me by the BSSC. The British Forces were very well looked after in Khartoum, and there were many opportunities for sports and recreation. We even had our own swimming pool.

British Services Sailing Club Medal

One memory that lives with me is that when King George VI died, our Steward met me at the gangway to the sailing club. He was in great despair, wringing his hands and saying, "Mombasa, Mombasa, what are we going to do? Our King is dead!"

At that time, of course, Sudan was a colony of ours, and he was quite right; it was a first-time experience for him.

In January 1953, our battalion was detailed to move to the Suez Canal, and I was selected to join the advanced party in order to merge the communications of my signal platoon with those of the Sussex Regiment's signal platoon, so this was goodbye to *Andromeda* and nearly the end of sailing in connection with the army. That is, except for my three years' Territorial Service when I was posted to the 2nd Battalion of the Parachute Regiment. They did their annual training camp in East Anglia, which gave me the opportunity of taking an extra week's leave and hiring a small yacht on which I could camp and sail the Norfolk Broads.

MIRROR DINGHY SAILING

Once I got married, money was in short supply, what with a mortgage to pay and children to look after, so sailing took a back seat until we went on holiday to stay with my sister. She was living in Wexford, Southern Ireland. She introduced me to a friend who had just built a Mirror Dinghy, sail number 1669, and named after the Australian challenger for the American Cup, *Gretel*, so I was able to enjoy some good sailing on the River Slaney and round Wexford Harbour. It happened that my friend was to return to Australia and could not take the dinghy back with him, so we bought *Gretel* and took her back home on the roof of our Triumph Herald. We sailed her at Hoylake on the Wirral Peninsula and had lots of good fun sailing in Liverpool Bay. We even took her to the South of France in 1968 on the top of the same car, with our three children inside and many gallons of petrol stored on the roof under *Gretel*, for this was the time of the national strike in France, and we had to make sure we had enough petrol to get us to the Mediterranean! It was all worthwhile, for we had a lovely holiday sailing in the Med.

Family and Mirror Dinghy

One year we took *Gretel* to the Menai Straits Regatta at Beaumaris; son Peter was helm, and I crew. It blew so hard that even the bigger yachts struggled but with my weight keeping the dinghy upright, Peter got first place! However, the next day was a race through the Menai Straits, via the Swellies, to Caernarvon. Owing to the strong blow the day before, the boom had put so much strain on the wooden mast that it was bent like a bow, and we could not get the mainsail to set properly. As a result, we came last, long after the fleet had all finished. After that, *Gretel* was given a 'tin' mast.

SAILING AT HOYLAKE

Next, we thought we could do with a bigger yacht. I was looking for a small cruising yacht that the family could enjoy, and we found *Gazabadaka,* a 20-foot Vivacity bilge keeler that would dry out on our Hoylake mooring, which, apart from supplying your own mooring anchors, was free. I went to night school to learn navigation and was taught by Captain Twentyman, a retired Master Mariner who had sailed tall ships round Cape Horn many times. He was very practical and thorough. I will always remember one of his sayings, "If you cannot find the mark you are looking for, look behind you."

Our first venture at sea was a cruise from Hoylake to Conway, about 38 miles into the harbour, along the North Wales coast and in sight of land. A good friend had a brother who was a retired Ships Captain, and he kindly agreed to come along with son Peter and self. All went well; we had a great sail and an enjoyable evening at the Conway Sailing clubhouse before returning to Hoylake the next day.

We had lots of fun sailing *Gazabadaka* with Hoylake Sailing Club and joined in the tidal series racing too—not with a great deal of success. We did manage 2nd place a few times, but we had better results when going further, to Anglesey and Puffin Island.

PUFFIN RACE 1976

On the 24th July 1976, we entered *Gazabadaka* in the Ten Foot Bank race from Hoylake to the buoy near Puffin Island, at the northeast entrance to the Straits. It is a race that is sailed on the Friday evening before the Menai Straits' fortnight at the beginning of August; the object is to encourage club boats to sail down for the Regatta.

All the required stores had been stowed aboard the Sunday before, along with plenty of cans of beer to give us a little extra weight in the right places! So, in the evening we only had to carry out the fresh food and extra water. As soon as the tide made enough water, the club launch collected all the crews for the various yachts and deposited the four of us onboard *Gazabadaka.* The crew comprised John and David, who normally crew with me, and Peter, aged thirteen, who joins us when home from school.

The time was nearly 20.30, and the race was due to start at 21h00; we had to be quick making sail as it would take us about fifteen minutes to sail to the start. The forecast had been good promising 2 to 3 from the northwest, but when I telephoned Liverpool Airport Weather Service before leaving home, they warned of rain starting at 21.00 and not clearing until midnight, with poor visibility during the rain. As soon as we got on board, the wind freshened, so we set the working jib, rolled two turns in the main, cast off, and immediately the sumlog recorded six knots. I noticed that some of the yachts had not reefed; true, they were larger than us, but I wondered how they would fare. As we approached the start line, a large sloop with a formidable bowsprit bore down on us and forced her right of way, nearly causing us to gybe, but as soon as she cleared our path, we headed up to the wind. The start gun went off, and we crossed the line, hard on the wind with the ten-foot bank buoy nearly forty miles dead to windward.

A good sea was running, causing waves that were confused by the shallow water of the East Hoyle Bank; the waves were at least six feet high, and all in all, the conditions did not favour a Vivacity 20. Still, we had a good start, and even though we sagged to leeward, we were still well in front, and the conditions were not helping the others much either.

Fifteen minutes after the start, the rain came, just as Liverpool Airport said it would. Down went the visibility, up came the wind, with blown spray from the white horses streaking across the sea. We must have been getting a force five, and if the wind strengthened any more, we would have to reduce sail still further, not much fun in that seaway. We were sailing *Gazabadaka* like a dinghy and paying off the mainsheet in the stronger gusts to stop her tendency to broach, but on the whole, she was still sailing well and riding the waves in great fashion, provided we took care not to take the larger ones on the bow when they would stop her. Just as the visibility closed, we could see the *Achilles Stormalong* screw herself up to windward and sail about ten degrees closer to the wind. Who would think we were in the same race?

Thirty minutes after the start, there was not a yacht in sight. However, through the murky gloom, I could just distinguish the strong sodium lights from the container base at Seaforth, and we were coming closer to the lights of a steamer in the Mersey.

Sailing a course of 0 degrees magnetic, we hoped to see the Flats buoy if we were close enough to see it, and shortly after, it came into sight on our port bow. At last, we knew where we were, so out came the beer—the crew has a habit of doing this, just when it is time to tack. The funny thing is that very little ever gets spilt! We tacked and set a course for the Horse buoy, which marks the limit of the East Hoyle Bank.

David remarked that last year when there was hardly any wind, we had withdrawn from the race, but here we were with wind in plenty charging on, the difference being caused by the forecasts we were given. Unlike last year this time, the weather should improve, which was a comfort to us in the prevailing conditions.

No sooner than we had discussed this than things started to improve; two yachts were seen crossing well in front of us and tacked onto the same course. The visibility improved, and what was that light in front of us? John passed up my list of local lights, and sure enough, it was the Horse buoy. On we went for HE 2, which, apart from the start and finish, was the only racing mark on the course, and it had to be left to port. HE 2 is the outer mark of the Hilbre Swash up the river Dee. Coffee laced with rum was passed up, and we began to sail past the two yachts that had tacked in front of us. The red light of HE 2 was in sight in front of us on the starboard bow, but I reckoned that the tide would set us out enough to pass it to port, and so it was. Peter flashed our Sharks Eye torch, and the powerful beam illuminated HE 2; we were on our way. David, our Spinnaker expert, retired below disappointed that his special art would not be required but happy at the prospect of a night's sleep.

The rain stopped, visibility became good, and with the drop in the force of the wind in the deeper water away from the banks, the sea eased. The lights of the Welsh coast were clear to port. We were sailing very well; the yacht, well balanced and almost sailing herself, was fairly charging through the waves in a phosphorescent glow. She seemed to sense we were in for a chance, sailing just free on the starboard tack going like an express train. The wind had gone round to the northwest a little; the powerful flash of the northwest light float was to starboard. I hoped that if we sailed just free with the jib full, the tide would take us past the Great Orme.

The red sector of the Great Orme's light came into view ahead. John took the tiller for a spell while Peter and I closed our eyes, huddled together in the cockpit. The red masthead light of a larger yacht astern fell lower and lower until only just on the horizon. The only worry was the two unlit buoys on our course; we could cause them serious damage at this speed!

Mesmerised by the swinging compass card and its light, John handed back to me and went below, eventually so did Peter. I thought the extra weight forward would help the trim of the ship, on we hurtled with the spray that came over like a warm shower, into the white sector of the Great Orme light. After passing the Orme, the first sign of a grey dawn appeared. John confirmed our course for the Ten Foot Bank buoy, a little closer to the wind now and crabbing sideways across the tide to the dark shape of Anglesey.

"Where is Puffin Island, John?" He checked our course again. "Yes," he confirmed we are right, and gradually we could see the hump of Puffin and then two small triangles of white sails ahead, making for the buoy. They were both faster yachts than us and finished twenty-five minutes before us. Then it was our turn to make for the finish. "All hands on deck," ready about. On the port tack, the tide took over and started to carry us back to the buoy, which was towering over us on the top of a wave. Ready about again and a longer leg on starboard, but still no luck. On the third try, we had the buoy abeam, stop watches in hand, we waited for the transit with the lighthouse, NOW we had finished: eight hours fifty-seven minutes and forty-eight seconds.

We sailed with the wind aft for the passage between the lighthouse and Perch Rock, watching the following yachts beat up to the buoy and seeing on the far horizon the masts of other yachts. Through the passage like a cork down a river we went, with the tide under us, and into the Straits. The contrast was immediate, smooth glassy water and still air, as we were sheltered by the Anglesey coast. The change from the evening before was dramatic and very enjoyable. We started the outboard, handed the sails, and motored into Beaumaris while my pipe was lit for the first time since the start. At 07.00, we dropped our anchor, just as the keels touched the bottom, and made a very big breakfast, followed by a good sleep for all.

At 10.15 the next day – Sunday – we recovered both anchors and set sail for home. It was a fine morning, and the Straits looked beautiful, with the background of the Snowdon range capped with low cloud. A gentle breeze of 3 to 4 knots pushed us on the way, no hurry and plenty of time to fish; the crew landed seventy mackerel before they were satisfied. I am pleased to report that all the fish were gutted at the first opportunity and stored in the freezer when home. No waste and some good meals. We had time to stop by Hilbre Island for tea while waiting for the tide to make before sailing round the Hoyle Bank to Hoylake. The *Achilles Stormalong* had made very good time during the night, so on corrected handicap, we finished second from the nine yachts that had started. Six crossed the finishing line; the others retired, including the large sloop which returned to its mooring on the evening of the race, having taken in too much water.

2nd Prize

In the winter, when the prizes are presented, we shall remember with pleasure and delight the time our small family cruiser forgot herself and raced like a thoroughbred to the surprise of her crew and many others. Well done, Vivacity 20.

oOo

During 1976 we had some very good outings in *Gazabadaka.* She did us fine, finishing 2nd in the Puffin race, 2nd in the

Liverpool Bar Lightship race, and 2nd in the All-Day Series of about six Sunday Races.

HELLO CHARLIE GIRL

After many happy years with *Gazabadaka,* we thought it was time we stopped sailing sideways and thought of a better yacht.

There were three Achilles 24' at Hoylake: *Stormalong*, *Serendipity*, and *Clairvoyant*; they all sailed well, and I looked to see if I could buy one locally and did find one for sale near Chester. What a find! An Achilles 24-foot triple keel named *Charlie Girl 2*, a real joy. David, John and I had lots of fun sailing her and racing at Hoylake in the All-Day Series finishing 2nd in 1977, 2nd in the Puffin Island Race in 1977, 1st in the race to Conway in 1978, 3rd in the Youngers Trophy in 1982. We also won the Liverpool Sailing Associations Cruising Award in 1988 and came 3rd in the Midnight Race to the Isle of Man in 1981.

1977 PUFFIN RACE

The 1977 race was completely different from the 1976 race. The weather forecast from Manchester Weather Office was for a steady breeze from the northwest throughout the weekend with maybe a little rain on Saturday afternoon, splendid, but unfortunately, there were only three boats that started. *Charlie Girl*, *Clairvoyant*, and *Keelie*. *Estrella* had been preparing to race but had experienced trouble with her Genoa furling gear and was a late starter; there was no sign of *Stormalong*, last year's winner, who we learnt later had been unable to start owing to a faulty rudder.

It would be a level playing field between *Clairvoyant* and *Charlie Girl*, both the same class and the same handicap. We did not have a very good start but had clear wind to starboard of *Clairvoyant* and soon made up the difference. The moon had risen before the daylight faded, so it was never really dark all night, and visibility was excellent. It was a perfect night for sailing; the only problem was the wind was against us, so it would be a long race. David took over while I worked up our position. I was mystified by a strong white light flashing 5 every 7 seconds; Peter was certain that it was the Liverpool Bar light, but in my notes, I had the Bar flashing 3 every 30 seconds (on our return home, a club member confirmed the alteration) lesson learnt, keep charts updated.

David had improved our position, so beer was passed round, John retiring behind a bottle of wine. *Clairvoyant* was on port, and had we held our course, we could have put her about; in view of the close finish, it might have proved a winning move! We continued on course 300C seeing the Bar to starboard and headed in the direction of the North West Float, which we could not locate. Normally when a buoy is difficult to find, it is my navigation at fault, but on return, the Coast Guard confirmed that the North West Float had been removed.

Gradually the sky was warmed with the first glow of dawn, and away aft, we could see what at first looked like the Isle of Man. Roger Doran, following in a Mersey Mylne thought so too, but on reflection, the angle would make the Lake District hills more possible; it had been a splendid dawn with beautiful light on the Welsh Hills

David pushed his head through the hatch, and I expounded on the beautiful dawn scene to him, but my remarkets were not well received. As a market trader, he retired, muttering about markets, and dawns any day. He reappeared to take over, and I went below to make some hot soup.

At 04.45, Peter spotted the North Constable buoy abeam to port, which, allowing for the tide, was where it should be expected. We held our course until 05.00 when we tacked again. I had expected the wind to back to the southwest around dawn and did not wish to stand out too far from the coast, and obligingly the wind went round until, with the sheets just freed, we could lay a course for the 10ft Bank buoy.

We now sighted *Clairvoyant* well offshore and slightly behind us. We were off the Orme at 06.00 with the wind still from the southwest. Things looked good, and it was reasonable to hope we might finish at about 08.00. Then the wind veered 80 degrees, and we had to tack out past the South Constable. John and I kept tacking with each shift of the wind trying in vain to improve our position, and, of course, the flood tide was now making progress difficult for both yachts. Any hopes of an early finish vanished, and it looked more certain it would be a close finish.

The wind changed direction again, and we were able to make a long starboard tack across Beaumaris Bay, all the time being set sideways by the tide. *Clairvoyant* was now windward boat and up tide might be able to close the distance, it looked touch-and-go to us right up to the finish, with *Clairvoyant* rounding the buoy three minutes and four seconds before us. After just over eleven hours, it had been a good race and an exciting finish. So, another second place!

We learnt later that *Keelie* had retired at about 08.00 with the flood tide against her and that *Estrella,* after a late start, had made it as far as Rhyl before the flood prevented further progress, and she turned for home.

We left Beaumaris on the next tide. Perhaps two night passages were not a good idea, but work called, and duty had to be done.

Following taking part in the Beaumaris Regatta in 1978, son Peter and self-sailed on through the Swellies to Caernarvon, then back to Beaumaris and round to Holyhead, intending to sail across to the Isle of Man. However, fog caused us to think again rather than cross a busy shipping lane in poor visibility, and we returned to Hoylake with a good spinnaker run.

The pleasure of sailing is hard to quantify. Sometimes it is only the discipline of a racing programme that gets you afloat. Your duty to your crew and other yachtsmen means you go out when weather conditions are such that you might stay at home, or who would turn out to start an overnight sail after a hard day's work? This reminds me of an overnight sail that Peter and I had back home from Beaumaris—not that we wished to sail at night, but the necessity was to get the yacht back and return to work, as so often happens. The experience went like this.

ST. ELMO'S FIRE.

This was not the most arduous, ambitious, or lengthy cruise, but perhaps the most potentially frightening passage that we have endured. My fifteen-year-old son, Peter, and I had sailed *Charlie Girl*, our Achilles 24, from Merseyside to the Menai Straits for the last week of the Regatta. Having taken part in the Hoylake Regatta on the Wednesday, we decided to take advantage of the first reasonable forecast to return to Merseyside; the tides were such that this would mean a night passage.

The 17.55 forecast on Wednesday 2nd August promised north backing northwest 3 to 4 for the Irish Sea, with occasional rain and good visibility. At the time of the forecast, visibility was poor and had been all day, so as a further check, we decided to visit the Liverpool Arms in Beaumaris and telephone the Coast Guard for a more detailed local forecast. A good excuse for a visit to the Arms if one was needed!

In the event, the telephone was out of order; however, we met a cruising friend who kindly offered to use his VHF to call the Coast Guard at Holyhead. We returned to his yacht while he called up the Coast Guard; they had no additional information to that of the 17.55 forecast, so we gave the thumbs-up, and he reported to the Coast Guard that we would depart at midnight arriving at Hoylake around noon on August 3rd. He gave full details of the yacht and crew and asked for the message to be passed to Formby, where we would confirm our arrival; we were very grateful to Desmond for his service. How wonderful it was then to have a VHF wireless. Now, of course, not only would you have a wireless but also a mobile phone, and radar, etc. How times have changed.

It was a pitch-black night, no moon, overcast, with slight drizzle as we departed from Gallows Point at 00.05, one hour after high water, with not a breath of wind. So, under motor, we crept slowly out, picking our way through the crowded moorings to the main channel. The night was so black that we had to use the torches to find the No. 10 channel buoy, unlit, as were many of the buoys.

Fortunately for us, we were joined by a local fishing boat who kept us company and picked out the channel for us; the steady thump of his diesel engine and his good masthead light were very reassuring. Eventually, we found the No. 2 buoy, which marks the turning point for the channel between Puffin Island and Anglesey and so out to sea. Suddenly the night had fallen quiet. There was no friendly thump of the fishing boat's engine and no masthead light. We had both heard the engine and seen the masthead light, and now there was no sound or sight of him anywhere to be seen; the Ghost ship had helped us down the channel, and we were grateful, but where had he gone? To this day, it remains an unexplained mystery to both of us.

However, the night had not finished with us. No sooner had we started across Conway Bay than came the 'mother and father' of a thunderstorm, the wind came up, but the sea was flattened by the heavy thunder, rain, and hail that poured down. Fork lightning, such as I had never seen, repeatedly struck and lit up the Great Orme's Head again and again, with great crashes of thunder. I felt tingles coming from the wooden tiller, and to make things worse, when I looked up at the mast, there were balls of blue fire running up and down the back stay. Fortunately, Peter was down in the cabin fast asleep, thank heavens, but missing all the fun.

I was very frightened. You hear tales of sailing yachts having their masts struck by lightning which results in the bottom of the yacht being blown out, and since we were the only object on the sea, that seemed a possibility. I pulled out my sailing knife, ready to cut the lashings holding the rubber dinghy, just in case. Those were the days before we had any means of wireless or mobile phone communication, so the prospect looked bleak. However, just as suddenly as it started, the thunder and lightning passed away, the forecast came right, and we had a peaceful sail to Hoylake. We arrived at midday and were **VERY** relieved to safely pick up our moorings!

The sequel to the blue balls running up and down the back stay, I eventually learnt, was that they are called St. Elmo's fire. As long as they are there, they will protect you, as they have the same electrical charge as the clouds. I am not prepared to put it to the test again, but something very mysterious was looking after us that night.

The experience has not put Peter off sailing; he has made quite a few offshore single-handed passages with success, in his own 29-foot Sadler, equipped with all modern gadgets!

MIDNIGHT RACE TO I.O.M.

In 1981, we decided to make a second attempt to join the Tranmere Sailing Club's Midnight Race to the Isle of Man. On the first attempt, the weather was poor, and the rough conditions caused our petrol tank stored in the aft locker to move and break the plastic outlet pipe from the bilge pump. With the yacht filling with water to the level of the bunks and John's homemade sponge cake in mortal danger, we turned round and sailed back to Tranmere.

On the second attempt, we had a crew of four on board: Peter, John Fielder, and Peter Bryson, a member of Hoylake Sailing Club and, of course, me. We left Hoylake as soon as the tide floated *Charlie Girl* at 16.15, with a forecast of wind west to northwest 2 to 3, maybe force 4 later, moderate visibility. All looked good, so we sailed via the Rock Channel, having dinner on the way. We entered the River Mersey, arriving at Tranmere at 18.15, ready for the start at 19.00. In those days, there was a very large number of yachts entered for the race and several different handicap classes. All went well until the wind dropped and the best of the tide had run, so we anchored outside the channel by mark C19 in company with a white Tomahawk named *Macaw,* which caught my eye, owned by Mike Warr and his wife, Fran. At 23.00, the breeze returned, up anchor and away we went, passing the Queen's Channel buoy 2 at 00.04. By 00.15, the wind was blowing southwest force 4 /5 occasionally 6, we stormed along 6+ knots on a course of 315 degrees magnetic arriving at Douglas, Isle of Man at 10.45, the barometer had only dropped a little from the start. Our corrected time was 12 hours 42 minutes, so we finished 3rd in our class. All the crew then enjoyed a good sleep.

The return from the IOM on Sunday was largely uneventful. We departed Douglas at 06.10 and motored out into Douglas Bay.

The forecast was good westerly force 2/4 with fog patches; we set the spinnaker on a course of 146 degrees. At times we were making 5 to 6 knots, a really good spinnaker run of 67 miles, in reasonable visibility, picking up our moorings in Hoylake at 17.55, about 11 hours 45 minutes for the return.

STRANGE TRANSITION

When does a small boat become a ship? I found that it happens after sailing to the Algarve…

Charlie Girl, my Achilles 24, was a childhood dream—strong, safe and fast. I kept her behind a sandbank off the blunt end of the Wirral Peninsular—with luck, she would float for two hours each side of high water and then dry out on her triple keels. A wise man, or a richer one, would have found a more comfortable mooring for such a treasure. With the sandbank covered, she was fully exposed to all the southwest gales. When the sun shone and the winds blew, she was blasted by the blowing sands. Not a perfect place by any means, but we were close by, and the mooring was free.

My wife Alison and I sailed the summer seas, we sailed when the winds blew, and the seas were rough, and the sky was grey. We sailed when the sun shone, and the sea was smooth and bluish. We sailed under starry skies with the coastal lights guiding us on the way. We raced with some success, round the cans and to Anglesey and the Isle of Man. Sometimes my little boat flew, spinnaker billowing, planing at 10 knots down the front of the waves. Often, we were cold, mainly we were wet, but always my faithful little boat brought us back to our moorings, safe and sound.

When we were older and a little richer, we started to dream of warmer climes with more certain sunshine, bluer seas, flying fish and a safe harbour. Just dreams to start with, but sometimes you must force them into reality. The question was: could my Charlie Girl carry me safely away from England, across Biscay and south to Portugal's Algarve and sunnier climes? Why doubt that such a sturdy friend would not serve us just as well as she always had?

One early spring day, with friends Simon and John, I sailed away from Plymouth Hoe against a backdrop of the Devon moors glowing in the late evening light. We headed down Channel hoping to pass outside the Isle of Ushant, but the weather gods had decided to tease us with an unsettled forecast for Biscay. A morning sextant sight gave us a position that allowed the alternative of seeking shelter in Brittany, so we altered course for L'Averwrac'h. But the gods had not finished with us and sent thick fog to make our sailing more interesting. In the days before GPS, radar, or chart plotters, you proceeded by dead reckoning, cunning and luck. At last, and thankfully, the tallest lighthouse in the world, Île Vierge, emerged through the mist, and we turned west along the coast looking for the entrance to L'Averwrac'h.

It was not a pleasant search. The sea was choppy, and we were on a falling tide; poor visibility made it seem almost dark. We found the entrance, but all around it were nasty jagged rocks like fangs covered with saliva. Our salvation came, or so we thought, in the shape of a fishing boat that we happily followed up the dogleg of a channel until he ran aground on a sand bank! All the pilot books had promised us pontoons at L'Averwrac'h. We found none and took a convenient buoy instead. The fog persisted all the next day, too thick to see the leading marks to find our way back down the channel.

By the following morning, the fog had lifted enough for us to make an early start and catch the tide through the Chenal du Four. We sped on under full sail with the tide under us and the engine ticking over. As we were spat out into Biscay on a glorious morning, the engine stopped. Investigations uncovered that the fine engine filter housing had become slightly loose. I had been aware that there was more water than I expected in the bilge, and it seemed I had carefully pumped out a full tank of diesel as it leaked into the bilge. It explained why the engine had lacked power and ran oddly. We had a spare can, but not enough to continue the passage, so up went the spinnaker and a wonderful downwind sail to Camaret. We stopped only long enough to refill our tank from a local garage, explain the reason for our visit to a charming lady customs officer, under whose window we had unwittingly moored, and we were on our way again.

Ch16 was quiet until suddenly halfway across Biscay, it sprang into life with, "small yacht behind, this is yacht *Me & You.* We have engine trouble; do you have an engineer?"

Well, it so happened that John was just that. Always worth taking along with you a qualified marine engineer; you never know when you will need one. Even with a fair old Biscay swell running, he was willing to risk the transfer, and we came carefully alongside, then stood off. *Me & You,* a British flagged vessel with a German delivery crew, had a fault with their fuel system. Our engineer was able to fix the problem, but unfortunately, they had so flattened the battery in their attempt to start the engine that there was no power left to start the engine. We recovered our engineer with no damage to either yacht, and *Me & You* could sail slowly on. We were pleased to see she had made port OK when we met up again in Spain.

Alone again, except for the company of shooting stars, whales, dolphins and sea birds, my little boat carried us safely until we made the Spanish coast. It was then we made the classic mistake. At dusk, we saw a lighthouse and made its characteristics fit the light we had hoped to find. Apart from nearly entering a blind bay, all the mistake cost us was a night's sleep and lots of frustration as we were caught up in the whole of the Spanish fishing fleet, who seemed to spend the hours of darkness turning their navigation lights on and off. GPS would have been wonderful. But we arrived at last. Then slept so deeply that even the knocking of the customs official failed to wake us. He kindly left us to slumber before returning later.

Onwards we went, with such tales to tell of Capes we had only heard of – Villano, Finisterre, Silleiro and Carvoeiro. It was my watch in the small hours of the morning sitting in the cockpit while my two companions were asleep below, the gentle warm breeze from the West carried us onwards it was a lovely night with a great canopy of stars shining brightly and for some unknown reason I started reciting the Lord's Prayer to myself, when I came to the ending the words; "For thine is the Kingdom, the Power and the Glory for Ever and Ever", those words had suddenly a very special meaning for me. Here was this very small spec of a yacht miles from any land in the Atlantic Ocean so small it was but a bit of dust, here in this wonderful Kingdom, with the mighty Power all round, what Glory, and the future was for Ever and Ever. Those words, so often said, now had a very special meaning for me and have done ever since.

As we headed ever south down Portugal's west coast, it became more and more difficult to receive the BBC weather forecast. When we saw a merchant vessel heading north, we called him up on the VHF to ask if he would kindly give us a forecast. It was very reassuring: "No problem for the next few days, while the high pressure is present. The only problem we have is this damned swell—we are rolling through 40 degrees."

We looked back, and, sure enough, his ship was rolling very heavily. We hadn't even noticed it because our vessel was so small that the swell had just rolled under us.

Finally, we arrived off Cape St. Vincent and turned east to enjoy the sunshine of Portugal's Algarve. Thankful for the journey's end, we reached Vilamoura thirteen days after leaving Plymouth. All those years ago, before the European Union, the official entry into a foreign port involved much paperwork. "Would the **ship's captain please attend**" was the request we were met with. I looked round – there was no one else, so it must be me, but what was all that about a ship? I was instructed to "Bring the ship's papers to the office". I had very few papers for my little boat but took what I had and, happily, all was well.

Sometime later, I was talking to an ex-Royal Navy friend at the bar and mentioned my new title of Ship's Captain. He enlightened me: "Boats are carried on ships: ships cross oceans." In simple terms, my boat had now been transformed into a ship.

Shortly after returning home to Merseyside, we had a rare and wonderful visit when the tall ships came into Liverpool following an Ocean Race. I can still hear the voice of the Radio Merseyside announcer calling out the names of these grandest of sailing ships as they came up the Mersey, and then he noticed that some of them were really quite small by comparison. "Ah," he said, "I suppose even the small ones are tall ships after crossing an ocean." With a lump in my throat, I could not help but think of my little old boat and agree.

We had many adventures and happy times sailing our ship along the Algarve coast, often in company with other members of the Vilamoura Cruising Club. But as the years wore on, we got older and stiffer, and the cabin got smaller and more difficult to be comfortable in. A fellow member suggested that we might consider changing her for a yacht with more room, but he said, "Don't you go and lose the performance that you have so enjoyed."

With this advice in mind, we started our extensive research for another yacht. After lots of consideration and some false starts, we found a Tomahawk 25 that measured up to all our requirements. We purchased *Keewaydin* while she was ashore on the hard at Topsham, and we have never regretted the decision. Sometime later, we put *Charlie Girl* up for sale. Although we were sad to part with her, the new owner keeps her in Faro, on the Algarve, so we still see her. We again had the pleasure of planning to take another small yacht out to Portugal and the sunshine. This time, Alison and I decided to take the scenic route via the rivers and waterways of France, but that is another story.

VILAMOURA

It is very interesting to keep your yacht in an international marina and meet so many wonderful travellers from different parts of the world. At that time, quite a few were resident in the marina for the long term; others were just passing through for a night, and some for a season or so, but we had quite a community and our own Vilamoura Cruising Club. Most members were British but not exclusively so. The club used to organise cruises along the Algarve coast at weekends to many of the beautiful harbours and sometimes a little further away to say, Saville. It also had a very good library, mostly books, but also comprehensive cruising directions built up by members over the years. On Sundays, when we were not cruising, races would be held, ending up at the clubhouse for fellowship and lunch.

I had not given much thought to yacht delivery, but it did play a big part in the coming and going, so it was not long before I was asked to be part of a crew to take an owner's yacht from Lisbon to Javier on the eastern coast of Spain some 728 KN miles away. The yacht was a Beneteau Oceanics 390 named *Osahoal*, and the two other members of the crew were my friends, Harry and John (I have changed the names for obvious reasons). Harry was a retired Chief Petty Officer in the Royal Navy with many years' experience of yacht delivery, and John was a retired police officer from Hong Kong, also a sailor with a yacht on the Algarve.

I flew out from Liverpool Airport, at the owner's expense, meeting the two others in Vilamoura on 16th July 1995. A friend gave us a lift to Lisbon, where we arrived at 15.10 to find *Osahoal* in Belem dock. Harry was keen to make a start immediately, so at 20.30, an attempt was made to leave the dock, but the yacht was moored bow to with a line from the stern to a buoy. Therefore, when Harry put the engine astern, with the wind blowing from the north at 25 knots, accidentally, the rope fouled the propeller, so we were stuck for the night.

The next morning there was no help from the local yacht club on the radio, so I was scrambled ashore, being the only one fit enough to do this. I was able to find a diver who would come to help, so by 11.00, the diver had cleared the prop with very little trouble.

No time was wasted; by 11.36, we had full sail set, engine running, and were sailing down the River Tejo at 6.5 knots in a southwest wind of force 2. Harry had cooked lunch for us—bacon and eggs if I remember correctly, but poor John coming out of the cabin lost his lunch in the cockpit! Shortly after this, we started watch—keeping the wind come up to NW 4/5, the engine was turned off, and we proceeded south at 6/7 knots. As darkness fell, we noticed that we had no navigation lights, so repairs were made to the lens with red and green tape and a new bulb fitted and on we went on a course for Cape St. Vincent.

I was sleeping in the fore cabin and was woken as we passed Cape St. Vincent by being thrown up in the air then banging back down on the bunk. The motion was so violent; you can only take so much before it is better to get up and dressed! We sailed well out from the Algarve and crossed the Gulf of Cadiz in the direction of the River Guadalquivir, making a diversion to avoid a tuna net that must have been four miles offshore. The wind came up to force 7 from the NNE in the afternoon with quite a rough sea, and Harry decided to head for the Bay of Cadiz and Porto Sherry marina for the night.

We left the next morning at 11.35 under full sail with an SW wind force of 2/3. Little did we know what was in store for us.

By the time we had passed Trafalgar, and we had a forecast from Tarifa of Force 8/9 with a levanter blowing strongly, it became prudent to enter the new marina at Barbate and join many more yachts that had had to do the same. Poor John had problems with his foot and had to go to the hospital on the 21st. They say a levanter will blow for three, six, or nine days. In the event, we left on the fourth day along with the whole fleet of yachts with an SSW2, entering Gibraltar at 14.10 the same afternoon.

It was wonderful to see the Union Jack flag flying high, do our shopping in Sainsbury's and have a pint of beer and an evening meal ashore.

In the morning, after refuelling, we departed. There was a good force 7/8 blowing from the west; the next day, we rounded Cape Greta and turned northerly for Cape Polas. Most of the sailing from Gibraltar had been in light winds, and most of the other yachts we saw were motoring under bare poles. I decided that sailing in the Mediterranean was not much to my liking. There are so many winds blowing from so many different directions that a gale can be upon you from a clear blue sky without any warning.

We sailed onwards up to Cape Nao then turned for Javea, arriving at 00.15 on July 29th. The next morning it was a quick shower and clean ship before handing over to the owner, who had arrived by car. We would then drive his car back to Vilamoura. So, we were ready to leave by 17.20 to arrive back in Vilamoura the next day. Then I had my flight home via Gatwick – again, the flight at the owner's expense – we were paid by the day. I cannot remember exactly how much, but I think it was $20 per day.

Return from Javea.

So, on the 20th August, we were ready to return to Javea. I flew into Faro where Harry met me, and we drove onto Tavira to collect John, then onto Javea where we arrived early next morning to find that the yacht had been damaged by a storm, had heeled over and smashed against the pontoon. The windows in the hull had been smashed letting water in so, we had to wait while the repairs were finished. Fortunately, the Spanish are very good at repairing yachts and did not keep us waiting long, and we were on the way on the 21st August.

It was a relevant uneventful return except for a very big thunderstorm on the night of 23rd August— 'all hands on deck' very heavy rain, and wind up to force 8 from the east. It was very difficult to reef the in mast main, and in the middle of all this, we saw a ferry steaming out of the heavy rain straight for us. We just avoided a collision, and by 06.00, all was in order. By 09.15, there was no wind at all, and we were motoring. That's the Mediterranean for you. The leach tabling of the genoa had come unstitched and would need repair when we arrived in Gibraltar.

Perhaps the best bit of the return was a wonderful dolphin display on the afternoon of 23rd August and the amazing show of shooting stars during the early hours of the morning of 24th August while heading for the Europa light. We were soon tied up to a berth in Gibraltar, and the genoa was sent to the sailmaker for repair.

We departed the marina at 10.15 on August 25th, whizzing through the Straits with a levanter behind us blowing east force 6/7. Near Cape Sagres, we picked up a dan buoy maker, which had to be cut free. Good job the wind was only WNW 3, so we went on round Cape St. Vincent up north with light winds to berth in dock Belem at 14.20 on August 27th. This time it was by bus to Vilamoura before catching a flight back to Gatwick and on to Euston; the only problem being that the last train to Liverpool had already departed, so for me, it was a night on Euston station before catching the first train north in the morning.

WINE RUN TO THE MED

The scenic route through France appealed to both Alison and me in order to take our newly purchased 21-year-old Tomahawk 25 from Topsham to the Mediterranean. Our previous yacht *Charlie Girl* had made the passage by sea, but now that we were both retired and over 65, we had more time available to enjoy the journey through the rivers and canals of France. Besides, it would be an interesting and learning experience for both of us.

Keewaydin craned in at Topsham

At Topsham, we craned *Keewaydin* into the water on a beautiful April morning, then sailed gently down the River Exe and out to sea, hoping to find some wind and have our first sail in her. In the event, we motored across a glassy sea to Brixham, where we spent a few days sorting things out. We discovered that the furling genoa would not furl, so we sailed on to Dartmouth to have it fixed.

We set off from Dartmouth at 14.00 to get the best of the Channel tides bound for Cherbourg. It was very cold with ice on the deck when we set off, but it was a lovely night's sail with a gentle following wind and nearly full moon. In mid-Channel, the yacht started to fill with water, and the bilge pump failed to work; the stern gland was leaking with no way of repairing it. I thought we were going to sink and have to use the rubber dinghy, but a desperate couple with buckets can work wonders—all was well when we found a matchstick had caused one of the valves in the pump to jam.

We finally made Cherbourg but not without being held back by a foul tide off Cape de la Hague, and once again, the engine would not start. Alison was watching the lighthouse going backwards when suddenly they turned the light out, and we could see the lights of Alderney getting closer! Eventually, the motor started, and we were able to make our way to the easy entrance to the Port of Cherbourg.

Amphibian craft at Tatouhou

From Cherbourg, we had intended to sail direct to Le Havre, but talking to others is always helpful, and another yachtsman suggested that we visited the charming port of St Vaast-le-Hougue. This was very good advice. We enjoyed our visit and even managed a trip to Tatouhou Island by amphibian craft and other areas in this attractive region and to sample the abundant supply of oysters and mussels.

After further trouble starting the engine, and with a favourable forecast after all the gales, we locked out of St. Vaast at 06.05 on a dark and cold morning, and when the sun came up, we had a very pleasant trip across the bay passing the remains of WW2 Mulberry Harbours on the way, and so we arrived at Le Havre. Now east of Greenwich, odd to think we were east of London.

Author at chart table

In Le Havre, we took the mast down to prepare the yacht for the canals by putting rubber tyres hung in sacks to protect the

Sailing wife

sides. We were held up in Le Havre, the regulations for the Seine compel you to make the 70-odd mile trip up to Rouen in the hours of daylight with no stopping on the way. In the early spring, it means there are only two or three days each fortnight when the tide makes this possible. Gales were blowing hard from the east, and we thought we would miss our slot up the river, so against all advice in the guide and pilot books, we asked for a passage to the Seine via the docks and entered the Tancarville canal. It worked well with all the bridges opening for us on the way.

The next morning, the locks were ready for us to lock out into the River Seine, but once again, the engine would not start. At the last moment, we got it going and shot out into the river where we enjoyed the most magnificent passage, pushed along by a near spring tide. At times we made 12 knots over the ground, past wonderful scenery. The banks of this majestic waterway are mostly well wooded, but we also passed high chalk cliffs. We shared the river with several ocean-going ships, and according to the pilot book, this stretch can accept vessels up to 80,000 tons. It certainly pays to keep a good lookout astern, as these monsters catch you very quickly and leave a great deal of disturbed water when they have passed.

We had carried the tide most of the way, and to our great surprise and relief, we arrived in Rouen at 18.30, comfortably within the hours of daylight. In fact, we had taken only seven hours and ten minutes to make the 60-mile journey. The next day we were joined by our friends John and Dagmar in their 9-metre

Catalac *Kiwanis*; they also had taken passage by the Tancarville canal.

Rouen is an interesting city with lots to see: a beautiful cathedral which they nearly lost in WW2; the city suffered from lots of bombing (mainly ours) but have made a very good job of restoration. The Joan of Arc church was a totally different modern concept, but we thought it beautiful, inspiring and notable for the 1415 stained glass from the church of St. Vincent.

Stained Glass window at Rouen

We had someone look at our troublesome engine and were advised that the trouble could be caused by a cracked cylinder head or a faulty gasket, poor timing of the fuel injectors, valve clearances, or a combination of all four!

We had serviced and checked the compression in Topsham, and the engine was running well when it started, so I rejected all the suggestions and followed through the fuel supply line, where I found that the simple answer was the fuel cut-off lever that you pull to shut off the engine was not retracting fully. After that, we had no more problems.

Soon we arrived at Amfreville and met the first Seine lock. These locks are very large, 180 metres long by 11.4 wide (590ft X 36ft), designed for ships rather than small yachts. After the first lock, the river changes its character and becomes more tranquil as it passes through beautiful countryside. Gently sloping banks and wonderful houses alternate with thickly wooded

Riverside Castle

stretches, and we passed beneath dramatic sheer cliffs on which stood chateaux, castles and churches.

Our entrance to Paris was sensational. We arrived on Pentecost Sunday when the banks of the Seine and the bridges were lined with Parisians in holiday mode. On seeing the Red Ensign on our yacht, they waved and called, "Welcome to Paris!" It was fantastic, and we felt we were part of a Royal procession! There can be no better way to arrive in Paris than to pass under all those magnificent bridges and to see the beauty of the city unfold before your eyes. The Eiffel Tower, the Arc de Triomphe, the Place de la Concorde, the Louvre. In the middle of all this, Alison was frantically trying to keep up to date with our position so we would know where the rule of the road changed, and which arch of the bridge to motor through and where the lights we had to obey were, and the reverse flow of traffic.

Entering Paris

Soon we came to the lock for the Paris Arsenal Marina. In very heavy rain, we entered the lock and rose up together with a large French motor cruiser, and as we rose up, Alison had the following conversation with the owner's mother.

"Where have you come from?" she asked.

"From Dartmouth, England," replied Alison.

"Sur la Manche?"

"Oui."

"***Mon Dieu!*** Not in this small yacht?"

"Oui."

"***Mon Dieu!*** Where are you going?"

"To the Mediteranee."

"***Mon Dieu!*** Where then to?"

"Espania, Gibraltar, and Portugal."

"***Mon Dieu!*** How old are you?"

"65!"

"Mon Dieu!"

By this time, we had arrived at the top and parted from the amazed lady.

The river above Paris, apart from a few industrial areas, continues to be just as beautiful. We paused at Fontainebleau to see the Chateau and do some shopping and then continued to our last Seine lock, the 'Champagne'. Locks are the danger points. Damage to the yacht or mast can easily occur. We had a near catastrophe in this one—narrowly avoiding severe damage. It ended with us turning round in the lock, making a quick exit. We then had to wait for two hours before there was space available for us to enter again.

After nearly 300 miles, we arrived at the canals; they are old and worn with creaking lock gates, dating back over three hundred years. We remember the slow, gentle and sedate progress between tree-lined banks with grey herons standing like statues patiently waiting for a catch, the fishermen there for the purpose, sitting quietly with blank expressions, next to a car with the boot always open! Above all, the overwhelming beautiful birdsong always present. But the calm is often broken by the frenzied action before the lock and the urgent need to visit the loo before you enter!

Aqueduct over the River Loire

We remember the friendships we made with fellow travellers, the villages, the inns and auberges, the pleasing simple meals, the taste of wine, the fresh croissants for breakfast and always the generous help freely given by the French, and again the birdsong.

We passed along the highest aqueduct in Europe, engineered by Mr Eiffel of Eiffel Tower fame, high over the river Loire nearly half a mile long. Then climbed to over 1200 feet on the Canal du Centre before dropping down and being spewed back into the River Saone at Chalon, returning to civilisation, marina berth, hot showers, supermarkets, and a few days' rest.

Then a dreary cruise along the Saone between high flood banks and on to Lyon to join the Rhône that sped us on our way past at times stunning scenery: vine-covered hills, beautiful cliffs and gorges, ancient and historic towns, castles, Roman towers. We stopped at Condrieu, asked for the wine of the region at a local restaurant, and nearly had our heads blown off by the beauty of the wine, too expensive for even M&S to stock now! Some of the locks on the Rhône were **enormous,** Then stopped at Avignon to dance on the bridge and visit the Palace of the Popes.

A Rhone Lock

Just before Arles, we branched into the Petit Rhône, about the size of the Dee at Chester, then joined the canal Rhône a Sete, through the Camargue, wild horses, the flamingos, pelicans, Romany styled weddings complete with shotgun volleys… the wide skyscapes to the distant blue of the hills.

We arrived at Sete with views of the Mediterranean at last, but unfortunately, family matters required our return home, so that finished our journey. We were amused at Sete Marina by the French, who arrived after the office had closed, obtained the number pass for the showers from another yachtsman, and departed before the office opened, one way of having a free night!

Now having done both, which way to Vilamoura? Across Biscay or through France? If you are in a hurry and pennies are important, then Biscay is the choice. If you wish to enjoy the taste of Europe, then next time for us it would be the waterways again, what a scenic route to travel and what an altogether unforgettable experience.

CRUISING WITH THE PENGUIN CLUB

My friend Alan Thomas introduced me to the Penguin Sailing Club, a group of sailors who join together to hire and sail yachts in many places that you would not normally have access to and at a price that you might not be able to afford on your own. The advantage is that you have an experienced crew with you and very good company.

My understanding is that the club was started by a group who had been doing research in the Antarctic, and when their tour of duty was over, they wished to stay in touch with each other, so they started by hiring yachts every spring, on the west coast of Scotland. The club just went on growing with many members that had nothing to do with the Antarctic. I did three cruises with them, and the first was from Dingle to Kinsale round the southwest coast of Ireland.

Penguins in Ireland - August 1998

The crews were free to make their own way to Dingle, but most took the ferry from Swansea to Cork, with a bus chartered from Cork to Dingle. Provisions were purchased mainly in Cork and topped up in Dingle. Three yachts were chartered: a Moody 44 with 9 crew, a Sigma 38 with 8 crew, and Benneteau Oceanis 35 with 6 crew.

It is difficult to distribute the food correctly between the yachts with the different number of crews, and our yacht was found to have more than its rations of sausages and bacon. We only just managed to sort this before war broke out, but we also had more Pringles than we should have had, and that was even more serious!

Saturday had been a long day and followed a night on the ferry without much sleep, so everyone was pleased to turn in, ready for an early start.

On Sunday at 06.00, we set sail out of the narrow part of the channel escorted by the famous dolphin, Fungie, who always seems to be in residence, and in light winds, we made slow progress towards Valentia then headed for the northern entrance into Portmagee channel and dropped anchor. We left at 12.15, having had lunch and left again by the northern entrance and headed out towards the Skellings carrying out the M.O.B. drill on the way. We held this course on port tack until the Skellings were ahead, then tacked onto starboard and were able to hold this tack right into the Kenmare River with a SW wind raising to 5 and steadily increasing rain. Finally, we picked our way into Sneem Harbour under lights even though it was only just turned 20.00. The wind was still increasing; the forecast for the next day was force 9.

Monday, with the forecast of force 9 from the west, nobody felt like being on a lee shore, so we stayed in harbour. There was plenty to do; some took the dinghies on a fishing trip, others spent time servicing the outboard motors. Some had gone ashore to explore Sneem returning with various goodies and were given a lift back by the kindness of the wife of the local landed gentry. One lady spent her time repairing sails while Clipper went to West Cove and back. It turned into a beautiful afternoon with the wind dropping. All water tanks were replenished, ready for an early start the next morning.

Tuesday, skeleton crews rose early by arrangement, so at 05.00, the yachts picked their way out in the early morning mist. Conscious of the need to be at Dursey Head to catch the tide, we arrived at Dursey Channel over an hour ahead of our target. We had the option of passing through the Channel, but with wind over tide, we opted to take advantage of the strong west wind and crack on out into the Atlantic, past Bantry Bay and Dunmanus Bay, and finally turning the corner into Crookhaven, where we were able to pick up visitors' moorings at around 17.00.

A very good day's sail with some rolly bits at times, but all stayed of sound mind and were enjoying it to the full.

I had never in my wildest dreams thought this could be such a wonderful Coast to cruise. There were beautiful views of the mountains and land from the sea and many varied and sheltered harbours to visit. No wonder it gets so many visiting yachts from France; it's their nearest and best cruising ground.

Those of the crews who had washed had to go and tank up with more water. Fortunately, in the process, they found a small Breton fish restaurant where we had our evening meal in two sittings. The proprietor could not believe his luck, nor could we, never expecting to have a fresh fish meal quite like this. We were now back on track and on time, where we had intended to be.

Fastnet Rock

Wednesday. We slipped our moorings at about 07.30 with an NW2-3 and headed out for the Fastnet Rock, passing the Irish Navy on the way and exchanging pleasantries over our respective bacon and egg breakfasts. It was a beautiful morning again, the wind rising to force 3 and giving us a brisk sail out and round and round and round Fastnet waiting for the final yacht to arrive so we could take pictures of all. It was so good to at last see this famous lighthouse. We were treated to a service visit of the maintenance crew, who were dropped by helicopter very efficiently, onto the top of the lighthouse, like something from a Bond film.

We headed back to the mainland via Goat Island and into Schull, where we were to put two crew ashore and pack them off in a taxi to travel with sails to Crosshaven to facilitate repairs. They would be picked up in Baltimore that evening. It was difficult to find a mooring in Schull, so we tied up to a trawler who was quite happy to have us.

We left Schull at 15.00 wind 3-4 and set sail for Baltimore, via Castle Island sound and Gascanane Sound, picking our way through narrow channels dictated by the depth of water passing to the south of Sherkin Island into Baltimore Harbour, where we tied up at the outside of the harbour wall, to pick up the remainder of the crew with the now repaired sail. Conditions this side of the bay were not good, and moorings were scarce and exposed. We made our way across to Sherkin Island and tied up to a pontoon in a very small marina, where the shelter provided a wonderfully balmy summer evening and a warm night.

Thursday. The weather was as the previous day, 3-4 bright and sunny. We made a latish start at 09.45 and went to visit Barloge Creek and Laugh Hyne. This is a nature reserve and an area of outstanding beauty, and not to be missed. Indeed, my brother-in-law, an Irishman who thought he knew the area well, had never heard of Lough Hyne, a salt lake slightly above sea level and accessed by a small channel by dinghy when the tide is right or by foot if not. We left Barloge at 15.15, having first explored some small caves near the entrance. Then we rounded the head of Castletownshend, where we anchored and fed ourselves but did not go ashore.

Laugh Hyne

We were away again at 18.00 and headed off to Glandore for the night, where we were able to find moorings and go ashore in the evening.

Old Head of Kinsale

Friday. Our last day, we left Glandore at 09.45 into another warm sunny day with wind SW 2-3. It couldn't have been better, and we headed well out to sea to clear Galley Head, and goose winged much of our way across to the Old Head of Kinsale where we were put onto the port tack and had a storming reach up to the river entrance. *The Sigma 'Magic Number'* with its new sail was flying. We were able to sail virtually all the way up the river, finally tying up alongside a French yacht in the main marina.

A suggestion had been made for an end-of-cruise meal which we were all in agreement about, but the concern was where could we find accommodation for all 23 of us, as most of the many eating houses were small but numerous in this gastronomic centre of Kinsale.

After some deliberation, we contacted the Blue Haven Hotel, possibly the largest (and most expensive) in town. To a man, all agreed to fund the meal, and we had a splendid evening.

The next morning, skeleton crews took the boats back to Castle Park marina on the other side of the river from where they would be returned to Dingle, and the coach arrived in time to take the party back to the airport or ferry terminal from where we sailed at 09.00.

I had some concern about sailing round the wet and windy southwest coast of Ireland at this time of the year or indeed at any time of the year, but I need not have worried, it was a lovely cruise in a beautiful part of Europe, with many inlets to explore.

WITH PENGUINS TO ÅLAND ISLES AND BACK 22/06/03 TO 28/06/03

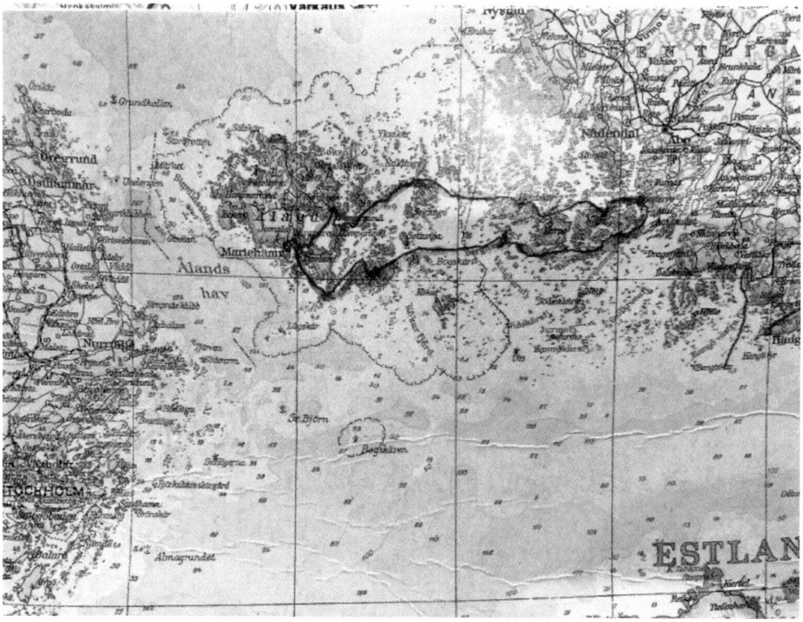

Map of Åland Isles

Åland Islands is a self-governing, Swedish-speaking province of Finland with its own flag. The province consists of more than 6,500 islands and skellies and is ice-bound for most of the year. The population is about 26,000.

The ice had only melted the month before we arrived. The Islands lie at the bottom of the Gulf of Bothnia or the top of the Baltic, between Finland and Sweden; they are low-lying, mostly of pink granite, which has been rounded and smoothed by the action of ice and waves, and they are covered with pine trees. At the time we visited, you have the midnight sun, owing to being 60 degrees north.

Fellow Penguin Club member Alan Thomas and I travelled to the new Travel Inn at Heathrow on Saturday 21st June, taking just four hours for the journey, having stopped for tea at the Hilton Service area.

The hotel was impressive. We had a very comfortable room, so comfortable that we considered spending the week there! We did a recce in the evening to find out exactly where the car park was for the morning, then had a good evening meal and an early night.

The Inn had promised breakfast at 06.30, and we were there on time, but in fact, it was not served until 07.00 which left us a little short of time, but we still had time for a full English breakfast, parked the car, and arrived at the Costa Coffee meeting place at the appointed hour of 08.20. Robin handed us our return tickets, the outward tickets having been deposited at the group check-in desk.

Having checked in, we proceeded through the screening process to the departure lounge. Our skipper, Phil Biggin, was called to one side, and his baggage searched. Unfortunately, Phil had moved his navigation package from the hold luggage to his cabin baggage at the last moment, and they found his knife and his dividers. The knife was taken, but he was allowed to keep the dividers, but even these fell afoul of the search at Helsinki.

While we were waiting for our flight to be called, the fire alarm went off, and the whole of the departure lounge had to be cleared. It was very busy, and there was semi-organised chaos; however, we eventually made our Finnair flight at 10.45, having experienced the normal 'hike' at Heathrow. We landed at Helsinki at 15.15 local time departing again for Turku at 16.10, finally landing at Turku at 16.45, where our buses were waiting to transport us to the marina at Aristo. It was an interesting journey of about one hour, giving us our first sight of the Finnish countryside, pine trees on pink granite rock.

We arrived at 17.45 at Aristo (Lat 60.14.56n Long 002 06 40e) in bright sunny conditions, the barometer reading 1012.6mb

By 18.55, all our luggage was stowed, and cabins allocated aboard *Linnea,* a brand new Beneteau Oceanis 331. The crew comprised: Phil Biggin, skipper, Charles Howell, mate, David Collinson, Alan Thomas, Rachel Roberts-Jenkins, and Corinne Slingo. We were then ready to join the crews of the other three yachts for our evening meal ashore, as we had not yet purchased our supplies. Settled down for the night to the accompaniment of loud giggles from the forecabin as the girls read Harry Potter's latest. Who switched off their cabin light?

The following is taken from the log over the next 6 days.

23.06.03

07.05 Barometer 1017.7mb, getting ready for breakfast ashore, the girls had found the numbers for the showers ashore.

09.45 Depart Aristo under sail at first.

12.10 Arrive Nagu. Shopping ashore for 3 to 4 days' supplies. Shopped at the supermarket; the girls had worked out a menu covering our meals and made a fine job of the shopping. They had volunteered to act as chefs for the trip, preferring it that way, in return for sailing instruction, and provided the lads did all the washing up!

15.00 Departed under engine then made sail as conditions allowed. The wind came up to 18 knots, and we tacked back and forth in the main channel. Busy with shipping to keep you on your toes. Found that the yacht's log was under reading by about one knot and bottom of the genoa was pulling out from the slot of the furling gear.

20.00 Anchored and rafted to another of our yachts, *Lija,* for dinner and drinks. Corinne had expertly cooked the smoked salmon that we had purchased earlier in the day.

24.06.03 Barometer 1016mb. Crew awake at 07.00. Corrine had difficulty pumping out the shower tray. We found this was connected to the 'spare' switch. Our anchors had crossed during the night when the yachts had swung. Still, we got them up without too much difficulty, but a great deal of mud!

10.00 under sail on a beam reach across the Sound to the Åland Isles at 6.5 knots. Found a good spot to anchor for lunch in the lee of the Kumling Isles. Lunch was cheese and ham omelettes, bread, and beer, etc.

14.10 Anchor up, and Skipper sailed off on a beam reach across the sound to Vardo at 6.5 knots passed by several ferries. One of the yachts reefed both genoa and main; we kept full sail with Corrine in her element on the helm.

19.10 while sailing the channels between the Isles, the Commodore (Ambassador to Finland) turned into a new channel of his choice only to find the route blocked by a bridge that had been put there since his last visit, so it was decided not to risk the clearance!

20.00 Anchored for the night rafted to Jonathan's yacht *Louise* in a lovely bay behind a small rock on the Island of Lumparland, in very calm conditions. Wonderful sunset/sunrise (at the same time) following a super day's sail. Can these super conditions, humour and fun last?

25.06.03 Barometer 1019mb. 06.30 Rise and shine, sunny, gentle breeze.

07.30 Anchor recovered after some difficulty but came up clean.

07.15 Depart under engine at first, then sail to Bomarsund. Here we enjoyed a bit of history. The Crimea war and the Charge of the Light Brigade might seem a long way from here, but this is where a very decisive battle was fought. The Russians had built a very strong and large castle here garrisoned by 40,000 troops. They thought the place secure and protected by all the

Bomarsund Castle wall

small channels, but unknown to them, the British had steam-assisted craft. The channels were all surveyed, allowing 28,000 French and British forces to be landed to take the castle, thus opening up the way to St. Petersburg, which the Russians could not face, so they sued for peace. The ruins still stand and are very impressive. Many of our party went swimming here; the only brave person from our yacht was Corrine. They all said it was wonderful but came back quickly.

10.00 Depart Bomarsund. We then enjoyed a very good sail across the Lumparn Sea with a following wind, into a small channel where we dropped the sails before passing through a swing bridge at 14.00 and so to the capital of the Åland Islands, Mariehamn, arriving at 14.50 and securing to a pontoon. The barometer now at 1026mb. This gave an opportunity, not to be missed, for the crew to shower, shop, and visit the museum ship Pommern.

26.06.03 Barometer 1027mb, sunny.

09.30 Move to pump out our holding tank; very important this as there is little or no tide up here.

Flotilla sailing

10.00 Depart Mariehamn for Kolm. Had a very good sail, passed the Island of Lemland and on for the Island of Foglo. On entering the channel, we came to wind and dropped our sails. Before this, *Liga* had been just behind us, but when the sails were stowed, we learnt that *Liga* could not start her engine and had turned away from the channel. We turned and followed in order to be of assistance if required. The skipper could not find the fault, so the *Commodore*, who had also turned, towed them to Begerby, the nearest harbour.

16.25 Secured at Begerby while efforts were made to sort out the engine problems. Most of the party enjoyed showers and swimming in the heated pool, and even a visit to the small museum followed by drinks on the veranda of the local restaurant. So, while we missed seeing more delights of Åland, there were positive compensations.

Mariehamn

27.06.03 Barometer 1027.8mb. Depart Begerby.

1300 Anchored and rafted for lunch at Salio, egg and cheese omelettes.

14.00 Anchor up, all clean. Very super afternoon sail across the sound, leaving the Åland Islands behind, the wind gradually increasing during the afternoon. We were sailing 'full and bye' and storming along until the wind came up to 25 knots. DSC, who was on the wheel at the time, could no longer stop the yacht from rounding up into the wind even with full rudder. First, we rolled the genoa, the more rolls, then one slab reef in the main until she became quite docile. We headed for a small island, and *Lija* found a wonderful anchorage for our last night at Berghann Island.

18.00 We anchored and rafted to yacht *Louise.* Dinner was pizza and salad, followed by drinks with our neighbours—Phil's Rum is some drink!

28.06.03 Returned to Aristo, good sailing at times between islands trying to make the best course to follow, and you might guess that we had problems with cables and bridges!

20.00 Back on base, signs of rain about, but we stayed dry. Eighteen of us enjoyed an evening meal ashore; the rest joined us for pudding.

29.06.03 Departed Aristo at 10.30, having cleaned, pumped out and fuelled the yacht. The buses took us on an interesting tour of the oldest city in Finland, Turku, before taking us to the airport for a perfectly timed flight home. Arriving back at Heathrow on time at 17.00 local time.

Crew

Note those of you who have laboured through this screed thus far and who are used to sailing in tidal waters will have noticed the absence of any reference to tides and currents. The reason being, there are none. I think if you really tried hard, you might notice a rise and fall of 10cm, but it could be an illusion. This all added to the enjoyment and relaxed sailing in these rather special islands. The weather helped too, but mainly it was the comradeship, the humour, and dare I say giggling amongst the crew that made this cruise so special.

WITH PENGUINS TO THE VIRGIN ISLAND

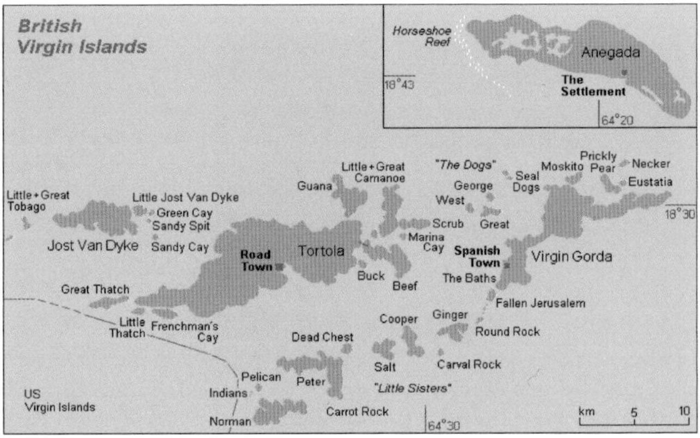

B.V.I. Map

At Christmas time 2005, Penguins gave details of a cruise to the Caribbean in February 2006. If my memory serves, the price for return airfares, two weeks' sailing, hire of yachts, and all food was about £600. I showed details to my son Peter, and he jumped at the idea, so our applications were made and accepted, and we could not believe our luck. Never in my wildest dreams did I ever expect to find myself sailing in those waters, a long way from Hoylake or Criccieth beach! The crews met up at Heathrow Airport ready to board the aircraft to fly first to Antigua, then transfer to an Inter-Island aircraft to complete the journey. The main airport connected by a bridge to Tortola, the main island of The British Virgin Islands, then by road to Nanny Cay marina to be allocated to our various yachts. I think my first surprise was to see a pelican standing on the pontoon quite relaxed, the first time I had seen one outside a zoo. Shopping for two weeks was the first priority, then in the evening, we all gathered for a meal. It was a very good marina with full facilities with showers, etc.

Baths Boulders

04.02.06. A lovely day. Lots of sun, so we departed Nanny Cay at 10.00, making our way to Drake's Channel. Around the SW corner of Tortola, we took care not to get close to the USA. Virgin Islands, and so on to Jost Van Dyke Island, where there are three good anchorages. This is the smallest of the four main Islands. The sailing conditions were excellent and remained so for the two weeks, just wish it could always be so perfect at home.

Beech fun at Anegada Island

The next day we sailed past Sandy Cay, where there was a lone palm tree, and one of the girls went into raptures about it, as she nearly always did when she saw a palm tree. Sailing on to Cane Bay where there was a very good resort, all facilities.

6.02.06 We left Cane Bay to Guana Island for the night. A very quiet place, before sailing over to the Baths on 07.02.06. This is a strange place with big boulders and worth a good exploring visit. We stayed sometime here before going to Spanish Town for the night, a bit more civilised! We sailed on round to North Sound for a trip ashore and visited the Saba Rock Sip n' Splash Club to buy some souvenirs. It is always difficult to know what to take home that is light enough for the aircraft and will not attract duty but still reflect the area's beauty. We spent the night there before sailing north out of the Sound, passed Neckar Island (the home of Richard Branson), and onwards on a broad reach to Anegada Island, which is only something like 28 feet above sea level at its highest point, not much more than a big sandbank really. It is 15 miles north of Virgin Gorda and made of coral and limestone, unlike the other Islands, which are volcanic. It is also surrounded by a coral reef that can make it difficult to get to and has been responsible for many shipwrecks.

Passing Necker Island

It is one of the most beautiful Islands, very peaceful with lovely sandy beaches and a population of 285 persons; a wonderful place to stay for longer than the one night we were there, but just avoid the hurricane season. On the 30th August 2010, Hurricane Earl visited it, passing about four miles to the north, but otherwise a real paradise. It is the second-largest Island in the group, with 15 square miles approximately and local fishing industry. To soon, we sailed back to the main group.

Enjoying the Sun

Cooper Island was our next stop for the night, having enjoyed a good sail back from Anegada. More swimming and snorkelling in gentle warm waters; life could go on forever like this, lots of sun, sailing, swimming and good company.

We called at Salt Island. This Island was a scene of a tragedy, for, in 1867, there was a massive hurricane when the mail steamship *RMSP Rhone* was alongside *RMS Conway* at the Great Harbour on Peter Island for bunkering. Captain Fredrick Wolley was uncertain about the falling glass and the dark clouds, but since it was October, the hurricane season was thought to be over. However, as a precaution, the passengers were transferred from the *Conway* to the unsinkable *Rhone*, and she set sail for the safety of open waters, but when the eye of the hurricane had passed and the next blow came, the *Rhone* was blown onto a rock off the point of Salt Island. She broke in half, and the boilers exploded with a loss of 123 persons. It is sad to think that the *Rhone* is now a tourist attraction and makes the most remarkable wreck to dive, swim, or snorkel over as we did, and found it very interesting all the while under the watchful eye of a barracuda!

Dead Island and Peter Island

I think we spent the last night of our cruise before returning to base, anchored off Dead Island near Peter Island. The evening will live in my memory forever; we had our evening meal in a marvellous setting while a steel band played all evening. It was an 'out of life experience'. There was, however, one great worry for the leaders: one of our party had gone missing. Confusion occurred as to which group he was with, then it was discovered he was with neither group, and a full search was made. He was not discovered until first light the next morning after a great deal of anxiety. The person had gone off to visit one of the yachts in a dinghy using the outboard. The outboard failed, as they sometimes do; he had no paddles and no means of alarm. Fortunately, he was blown across the channel onto another island, and all ended well. A lesson to learn.

And so, it was back to Nany Cay Marina for the very last night, clean the yachts, then a crew evening meal, and departure next morning by local plane from Tortola airport to Antigua, then back to Heathrow. What a wonderful experience, and memories forever.

LAST GASP

My son Peter keeps his beautiful Sadler 29 at Gosport on the Solent and kindly asked me down for some sailing with him. It was a little difficult to find the time suitable for both of us, but we did, little knowing that it was Cowes Week, but it made little difference to us; in fact, it enhanced the weekend seeing all the racing craft. We left Gosport and battled our way mainly against the tide to Yarmouth for the night, taking a buoy outside the main harbour and a motor-taxi to shore for the evening meal. Then next day, we headed out to The Needles.

The Needles

The wind and the tide were right for a trip round the island. St. Catherine's point was clear, but Peter needed to do some work at the masthead while there were two of us, so to Cowes we sailed to do the work and have lunch.

The Needles

All went well with the mast work, and it was good to have Peter down on the deck again, so we sailed from Cowes and back to

Gosport, having taken care on the way not to upset the racing yachts, but enjoying watching them all the same, which was a bonus.

Racing during Cowes Week

At that time, Peter's yacht *Blue Shadow* was moored to a floating pontoon in the river, so it meant using the dinghy to go back to shore. On getting out of the dinghy, I tripped and fell in the water, perhaps a fitting end to all the years on the water; I had to end with a splash!

Mast head repairs

Printed in Great Britain
by Amazon

69734950R00037